The Thoughts inside My Head

The Thoughts inside My Head

Are Scarier than the Monsters under My Bed

Sara L. Pogue

iUniverse®

THE THOUGHTS INSIDE MY HEAD
ARE SCARIER THAN THE MONSTERS UNDER MY BED

iUniverse books may be ordered through booksellers or by contacting:

iUniverse
1663 Liberty Drive
Bloomington, IN 47403
www.iuniverse.com
844-349-9409

Because of the dynamic nature of the Internet, any web addresses or links contained in this book may have changed since publication and may no longer be valid. The views expressed in this work are solely those of the author and do not necessarily reflect the views of the publisher, and the publisher hereby disclaims any responsibility for them.

Any people depicted in stock imagery provided by Getty Images are models, and such images are being used for illustrative purposes only. Certain stock imagery © Getty Images.

ISBN: 978-1-6632-3817-7 (sc)
ISBN: 978-1-6632-3818-4 (e)

Print information available on the last page.

iUniverse rev. date: 04/21/2022

To all the poets who
said they couldn't but did.

My mind is full of thoughts
I don't know how to say.
All grey and full of decay.

A full-blown cast away.

My sanity frays from reality
when the world has no guarantee.

Treat the earth with kindness.

I am flawed,
I am human,
I am sad,
I am learning,
I am me,
And I will never apologize for that.

I owe you my life for
being the person
I needed but didn't want.
For refusing to leave my side.

The thoughts of bullets and bruises
leave when I think about you.
The thoughts of knives and scars
appear when I think about him.

I'd rather think about you.

The dark inside us shines
brighter at night.
It's where thoughts come out to play,
while the madness silently slips out.

Instead of sheep,
I count the monsters under my bed.
All the while listening to the
sweet symphony of the demons
inside my head.

Humanity was over when the bigots
plead insanity for killing
the divergent but not yet
emergent beliefs of others.

My monsters look a lot like me but with the thoughts of my former self.

I have more good thoughts than bad, but my bad thoughts are what will take me to my grave.

This war in my mind has
you as its leader.
The scars on my body have
me as the soldier.

I'm drowning in the
ocean of my mind,
In the sea of my regrets
and disappointments,
Where I see a sunset.
Too far to reach,
Too dark to be joyous.
I stare into the empty
abyss of water,
Until all I see is my own reflection
Trying to destroy us.

Silence is where the heart finds
its passion and the mind finds
its happy place.

He's pretty but toxic, so
handle with care.

She's fragile but sinful, so beware.

If home is where the heart is,
I am lost.

I'm not sure if we're forever,
but right now is good enough.

They say you need to love yourself
before you can love someone else.
But I found love in me
after I found it in you.

Kiss me under the stars,
while the wind whistles our names
and the moon calls out to the sun.

I love you.

You were the sun on my rainy days, but now you're the *thunder*.

Until you,
I didn't know me.

My love for you was like a
thousand doves trying to
flutter out of my heart.

Loving you was like adding
a jalapeno instead of a
lime to my tequila.

Spicy.

No one told me it hurts
this much to love.

My soul will forever
be intertwined with yours,
as they dance through the night
under the stars.
Happily in love.

Love is like a jigsaw puzzle.
One you have to build,
paint, and then
put together just to find out
that you're missing a piece.

I am not asking for forever,
as I know your love is stronger when
you focus on today.

I am not asking for tomorrow,
just love me for today, and I promise
to love you just the same.

While my head is on his chest,
I can hear his heartbeat
like a base drum.

Music to my ears.

Broken hearts will heal over time,
Just like bones.
Except you can't fix a
heart with a cast.

Try tequila.

You know how to put
my broken pieces
together to make a
misshaped puzzle.

Thank you for fixing me.

Crazy is the happy we want to be.

I found you in the tearstained
pillowcase I never washed.

It still smells like you.

Beauty is oceans deep.
Asleep in the colours of our eyes,
It never dies.
This beauty inside us.

I sit outside,
wine in hand,
and wonder what it's like to fly.

I lay in bed with love in my heart
and you in my arms.
Chest to chest and lips to lips.

Forever yours.

I am no longer that weak little girl,
For your love has made me stronger.

We are born like roses.
The symbol of love in the form of life.
But we grow into the thorns
that we try to hide.

We lie our way into toxicity.
We are no longer the
flowers that grow
in spring but the rain that
pours on cloudy days.
We are afraid to let our
petals bloom again.

If you were to fall ill,
I would give you half my heart.
For all of it is filled
with love and good thoughts of you.

His body was like an avalanche. Always tumbling from the top and starting from within.

Without you,
I would have nothing to write about.

You are my muse.

I write to know that my mind hasn't gone into total darkness, and that I am still alive.

I am calm.
Considering what's going
on in my mind.

I'm tired of losing myself to find you.

For once, I choose me.

I don't know who I am.
Maybe if I did,
I would hate myself a little less.

Kindness and love will
save humanity.

My life would be empty
if I didn't love you.

You were my superman,
Until I knew what an addiction was.

Former daddy's little girl.

You chose alcohol over me,
So I'm sorry if I choose
everything else over you.

If you grow up with an
alcoholic father,
You grow up with an alcoholic
and not a father.

You always took all the punches.
Even if they were aimed for me.

From your thankful little sister.

Five years apart,
But best friend at heart.

Sisterly love.

You lie like it's a full-time job.

My mom, my angel, my rock.
Through cancer, abuse,
and much more,
you never give up hope.

I strive to be like you.

I never understood how
a father could hate
his creation, then lie about loving it.

Because of you, I now know what *not* to do with my life.

I, subtly, thank you.

I'm in a pit that I can't get out of.
It keeps getting deeper and deeper,
It's like quicksand except
the only things
I'm buried in are my own thoughts.

I dwell on my past like I
forget I have a *future*.

Anxiety.

I crave you like I crave ice
cream on a sad day.
But like dairy,
You're bad for me.

Hold me like you're leaving forever.
Then stay.

You embrace change the same way
you embrace your addiction,
By ignoring it.

I'm sorry, Dad,
That we weren't good
enough for you.

Fall asleep with me on
the mountain tops,
while the sun says goodnight
to the moon and
the stars shine so bright
our shadows cover the
trees below.

I never thought I would be afraid to look at my own skin until you touched it.

I aspire to be the woman my
mom always thought I could be.

Take me to the ocean, and bury
me in the waves of my past.

To Dad:

Life can be wonderful
and colourful and fun.
Please put down the bottle and look.

I am strong because you
thought I was weak.
You were wrong.

I write the words I
don't know how to say.

Your scars match my scars.
Let's paint them with stars
and watch the sky dance
on our skin.

I don't need a crystal ball
to see you in my future.

I will never stop flirting with you.

The love we have in our hearts
will shake the earth to its core.

My life could have turned
out so differently.
I'm thankful it didn't.

Look into the stars and
you'll find peace
in the artwork of the constellations.

Your addiction used to be
a coping mechanism.
Now you are your addiction.

I hope your addiction fills the hole
that your children's love
never could.

I'm tired of losing friends because of the thoughts inside my head.

End the stigma.

You don't have to hit
someone to bully them.
Words leave scars too.

You don't think you have a problem,
And that's the problem.

That drink was the first mistake
I made that night.
Trusting you was the second.

This world scares me the same way
society has scarred me.

Anxiety and depression are like
a ship called Fright, going into
a whirlpool of loneliness.

My bed.
Your voice.
That book.

My happy place.

Depression isn't an enigma,
But we're the reason
there's a stigma.

The monsters inside are
not ready to hide.

My own expectations are
what started it all.

Create your own path.

Patch up your heart,
drink some tequila,
and walk it off.

They're not worth it.

Like the clouds,
I move with the wind.

If shoving me into a wall made you happy,
I hope you are never happy again.

I mean that with love.

You stole my heart and
tied my feet together
so I could never get it back.
My heart is gone.
Forever and always yours.

I lost you in all the I love you's
when you realized you didn't
feel the same.

My anxiety pops up like
a jack-in-the-box.

Randomly.

My thoughts scare me
when I'm alone.

Divest from the world,
invest in yourself.

His toxicity is as bitter as
the alcohol he drinks.

May my love find yours,
wherever you are.

I loved you once.
I miss that.
I miss you.

Don't you?

I don't cry over hurt
feelings anymore.
I bleed it over paper
until the red turns
into the words I can't
say but only feel.

The violence in that
house was as silent
to the outside world as
the narcissism
was to the narcissist who lived in it.

I changed my mind,
but you turned a blind eye.

I didn't say yes.

My mind is like the sky,
an endless abyss of nothingness.
But it is also like the sun,
Bright and dangerous.

I'm like the ocean, and
you're like the sand.
Together we make
quicksand to drown all
the people who said we
would never work.
But we are artwork: rare and
perfectly imperfect.

In our society, we are treated
like a commodity.
We are bought and sold
like the cure to a cold.

But we all matter.

If beauty defines us, why
not make it unique
in an expressionistic-form-
of-love kind of way?

I am woman, stronger than that fist you threatened to hit me with.

My story is not over.
It's just beginning.
Be prepared.

Thank you.

For reading this part of my soul.

To everyone who believed in me
and to everyone who hurt me.

Thank you for my story.

CPSIA information can be obtained
at www.ICGtesting.com
Printed in the USA
BVHW041019260522
638158BV00005B/26

9 781663 238177